Newfoundland and Labrador

*Poetry, Interesting Facts, Culture,
Traditions Old Dittie and Sayings*

Written by Award Winning Poet
Margaret High

Copyright © Margaret High 2020
All rights reserved. The use of any part of
this publication reproduced, transmitted in any
form or by any means electronic, mechanical,
photocopying, recording or otherwise stored in a
retrieval system, without the consent of the
publisher, is an infringement
of the copyright law.

Self-Published
Margaret High
Cambridge, Ontario

For more Information
E-mail: margaretehigh@gmail.com

Facebook Pages
@authormargarethigh
@myjustncase

ISBN 978-0-9809826-6-4

Dedication
I dedicate this book to my husband, my family,
and my friends; to my Toastmaster club
and my "special" friends who support
and encourage me. Because of my
upbringing on Bell Island, Newfoundland,
I hold a lot of my precious memories.

Table of Contents

Newfoundland People 1
HISTORY
  Newfoundland's First Settlers 2
  The Viking 3
  The Last of the Beothuk 4
  In the Beginning 5
  Amelia Earhart and Harbour Grace 6
  The First Settlers of Bell Island 7
  The Innu 8
  The Brave Five Hundred 9
  The Blue Puttees 10
  The Royal Newfoundland Regiment 11
TRAGEDIES
  Helicopter Taken by The Sea .... 12 & 13
  Bell Island Tragedy 14
  The Maryann and Somerset Disaster 15
  The Garland and the Golden Dawn .... 16 & 17
  Lost to a Watery Grave 18
  St. John's Fire 19
THE CUSTOMS
  A Newfoundland Meal 20
  Bonfire Night 21
  Janni 22
  Valentine's Day 23
  Mummers 24
  Nanny's Homemade Bread 25
  The Capelin Is In 26
  Smugglers 27
  Nanny's Fancy Apron 28
  The Blueberry Patch 29
  Clothesline 30
  The Squeeze Box 31

Table of Contents

MYTHS & LEGENDS
   The Newfoundland Dog 32
   The Woman in White 33
   A Tale About the Micmac and the Beothuk.................34
   The Fairies 35
   The Oryrog..36

THE PEOPLE
   Treasures of the Sea 37
   Woody Island 38
   This Old House..39
   Why Does This Island Draw Me Home.......................40
   They Wait, They Wait...41
   The Old Lamp..42
   The Miner ....43 & 44
   The Music...45
   The Old Kip..46
   "Bell" The Moose..47 & 48
   Back In Time 49
   Back Then...50
   Remember When 51
   Her Eskimo Friend 52
   The Lighthouse 53
   The IceBurgs 54
   The Battered Old Squeeze Box 55
   My Boat...56
   The Old Fisherman...57
   Newfoundland Place Names.................................58 & 59
   After The Mines 60
   The Mines Are Closing 61
   Terrorist Attack 62

OLD DITTIES 63

OLD SAYINGS ....64 & 65

> Everyone who's ever visited Newfoundland has always commented on how friendly thepeople are. Friends of mine loved the genuine hospitality they felt there.

NEWFOUNDLAND PEOPLE

Newfoundland people are gracious
And as friendly as can be
They'll invite you in for a mug up
Then offer a cup of tea

They will spread the table proudly
You're made to feel at home
They'll share their food so willingly
'Stranger' is a word unknown

They are resilient close-knit people
They come together when times are tough
Admired by the rest of the world
Simplicity seems enough

They are genuine accommodating people
Come in and make yourself at home
A phrase that's so often used
"In Newfoundland, you're never alone"

HISTORY

Humphrey Gilbert claimed Newfoundland for England in 1583 and the first year-round settlers arrived in 1610. France contested England's claim and Newfoundland changed hands several times.

NEWFOUNDLAND'S FIRST SETTLERS

Ever since the sixteen century
Fishermen have been lured to our waters
Some Europeans have migrated there
Bringing wives, sons and daughters

Queen Elizabeth 1 laid claim
To be part of England in sixteen ten
John Guy led these first settlers
To our New Found Land

The attempt to colonize was not easy
There were hostilities along the way
Fighting over ownership of properties
But they stood fast and stayed

Settlers would trade with New Englanders
As they came to Newfoundland
Carrying woollens, salted meat and rum
To trade for salted cod, fish oil was in demand

King Charles passed the Navigation Act
To try to stop the surge of smuggling
However, this task was not an easy one
It took years and years of struggling

There are over half a million people in Newfoundland today
With courage and determination they built their frontier Yes,
the first settlers of Newfoundland
Truly were the first Canadian pioneers

> It's been said that Vikings sailed the shores of Newfoundland and Labrador in 986 AD. Who are we to dispute it?

THE VIKINGS

It was long believed in Newfoundland
Many many years ago
Even though scholars weren't sure
It was the merging of the new and old

These Vikings they called warriors
With their paganistic ways
Worshiping so many gods
Setting churches and monasteries ablaze

Their open boats propelled by oars
Sailing them over the open seas
Raiding taking and pillaging
Settling in the land of trees

A Scandinavian named Bjarni
Set sail to Newfoundland and Labrador
They found and settled near L'Anse aux
On the island's north-eastern shore

Archaeologists found the remains
Norse structures of this colony
Five hundred years after they'd left
There are recordings of their brief stay

> The Beothuk people became extinct in 1829 when Shawnadithit, the last known Beothuk, died in St. John's, Newfoundland.

THE LAST OF THE BEOTHUK

*She was born near a lake in Newfoundland
In the year of eighteen hundred and one
Her tribe was called the Beothuk
She was starving, alone and shunned*

*Her people hunted for shelter and food
Some would barely survive
The sickness that the white man caused
Would wipe out most of her tribe*

*The white man hunted them down
Thinking they were nothing but thieves
Trappers and furriers attacked them
Just to keep them away it was believed*

*Shawnadithit was the last known Beothuk
She died in St John's in eighteen twenty-nine
There is a statue in her honour
In Boyd's Cove the last of her kind*

Many people have tried to claim Newfoundland, but it remained part of the British Colonies until 1949 when it joined the Confederation with Canada. Labrador is an adjoining mainland coastal region.

IN THE BEGINNING

They say Vikings visited Newfoundland
Many centuries ago
And briefly established a settlement
In Newfoundland L'Anse aux Meadows

In fifteen thirty-five
Jacques Cartier sailed through the Cabot Strait
Humphrey Gilbert claimed Newfoundland
Becoming a part of England by its Head of State

In fifteen eighty-three
The first round of settlers arrived
Newfoundland changed hands several times
From Britain to France they contrived

In sixteen ten a Bristol merchant
Brought settlers to Conception Bay
By sixteen twenty-one
Many colonies were on the way

In seventeen eighty-three "French Shore" was redefined
It then included the west coast
Followed by Hudson Bay forming
Bringing fur trade and fishing to the outpost

Spain and England claimed our shores
Portugal and France had ships on our banks
Many tried to take control
But the British held the ranks

We stayed under British rule
Until nineteen and forty-nine
When we joined one with Canada"
A new found land" was redefined

> In the year nineteen thirty-two, Amelia Earhart left Harbour Grace to set off across the Atlantic. She stayed briefly at Archibald's Hotel. Many years later my mother worked at that same hotel.

AMELIA EARHART AND HARBOUR GRACE

Who would have thought
In such a small secluded place
An aviation historical event
In our own little Harbour Grace

It took place in May of thirty-two
Across the Atlantic, she wanted to fly
Amelia Earhart was to be the first woman
Not many could understand why

Onlookers anxiously waiting
To see her off or to just touch her plane
Never suspecting for a moment
That they would never see her again

While waiting for a mechanical check
She retired at Archibald's Hotel
After a rest and a thermos of Rosie's soup
She was relaxed and feeling well

Amelia set off to cross the Atlantic
It was a beautiful sunny day
And the little town of Harbour Grace
Was there to see her on her way

> It's said that Bell Island had the richest soil - more so than any other part of Conception Bay. It was this richness that brought one of the first settlers, Gregory Normore, to the Island.

THE FIRST SETTLERS OF BELL ISLAND

They first discovered iron ore
In eighteen ninety-three
This rich little island in Conception Bay
Surrounded by the sea

The beginning of settlers on Bell Island
Goes back to seventeen-thirty nine
When Gregory Normore made his way
Away from his native isle

Settlers were fascinated by what they saw
There were cargo ships from East to West
Laden with spices, tobacco, molasses and rum
Tasting of our foaming ale. "Ah" it was noted the best

Bell Islanders were hard-working people
Forefathers were English, Irish and Welch,
The early settlers soon realized
They unlocked treasures of mineral wealth

High cliffs gave an added shelter
From the cold northerly winds
Fish for drying spread along the sandy shore
Comfortable living for Gregory's kin

> The Innu people descended from Algonquian-speaking hunters. One of the major communities in Labrador is Sheshatshiu on Lake Melville. Today the Innu are represented by the Innu Nation.

THE INNU

Newfoundland and Labrador
The home to many aboriginal
The Inuit, Innu, Micmac and Métis
They truly are the originals

The Innu is known as Naskapi-Montagnais Indians
And the word Innu means "human being"
The language is called Innu-aimun
Relying on hunting for their feeding

They lived in tents made of skin
Small bands in Quebec and Labrador
Caribou was the source of food and clothing
They were explorers, traders and so much more

With the animals slowly disappearing
Finding themselves without food and supplies
This led to disaster for the Innu
A culture could be jeopardized

In the nineteen fifties came assistance
Changing their way of life
Separating children from parents
Causing them pain and strife

Once a proud and independent people
Cut off from the only life they've known
Now shunned and looked down by others
Still searching for a place to call home

> This was taken from the First Five Hundred, also called the Blue Puttees. The Church Lads Brigade was a big part of Newfoundland.

THE BRAVE FIVE HUNDRED

Two recruiters came to the CLB
They enlisted five hundred brave young men
The best of the best to join the Blue Puttees
Leaving behind their family and friends

They crossed the broad Atlantic
And entered into the "Hobs of hell"
On the bloody beaches of Suvia
They were among the first that fell

They came for the last July drive
Down in trenches prepared to die
Next morning only a handful survived
Never once questioning why

They celebrate these brave young men
Every Memorial Day
And remembering when family and friends
Watched as they marched away

Originally formed in 1914, the Newfoundland Regiment, as it was known at the time, consisted of what many refer to as the "First 500" or "The Blue Puttees" about the blue leggings worn by the men.

THE BLUE PUTTEES

They were called the Blue Puttees
Because of their blue wool-trimmed pants
They wore them with such pride
They were distinctive brave and confident

They first battled in Egypt
In the year nineteen and fifteen
Travelling from battle to battle
Many wars these brave Puttees had seen

They were the best and the brightest
The bravest there was no doubt
Many battles they had fought
They stayed and toughed it out

The Regiment was formed in 1914
The First Five Hundred they were also called
The King of England bestrode the Royal
So valiant were their efforts to answer the call

They celebrate every first of July
The fighting Newfoundlanders
Remembering with honour and pride
The soldiers and their commanders

> So valiant were the efforts of the Newfoundland Regiment that the King of England bestowed on them the title of the Royal Newfoundland Regiment.

THE ROYAL NEWFOUNDLAND REGIMENT

They say it was formed in nineteen-fourteen
And reformed in forty-nine
It was part of the British Force then
Brave volunteers waiting in line

On the outbreak of the Great War
Many were called to fight
These courageous Newfoundlanders
Must have looked an amusing sight

There were no suitable uniforms then
With ingenuity, they made their own
Knitted woollen caps, bottom and tops adorned in blue
Blue Puttees was how they became known

They were involved in the Battle of Gallipolis
Beaumont Hamel and Cambria
Newfoundlanders displayed their great courage
Some were slaughtered on German barbed wire

They were called the First Five Hundred
They were "better than the best"
Dead men can't advance any further
Major General Cayley did attest

Yes those brave Newfoundlanders
They fought in many wars
They've earned their honour and respect
And remembered for so much more

TRAGEDIES

The tragedy of 2009 inspired me to write about the Cougar flight 491.

HELICOPTER TAKEN BY THE SEA

On March 12th, 2009
Aboard the Cougar flight 491
Never suspecting for a moment
This would be their last run.

Eighteen people left that day
On their way to Hibernia and the Sea Rose
Something terrible happened
Why? Only God knows

The sea took them home that day
All but one have died
This tragedy affected so many
Hundreds said their good-byes

There was Matthew, Peter, Colin and Keith
All came from old St. John's
Wade and Burch were from Fortune
May their memories always live on

There was Corey who lived in Paradise
Thomas and Tim were from BC
Gregory came from Outer Cove In
our hearts, they will forever be

There was John from Deer Lake
And Gary from Conception Bay
Ken came from Nova Scotia
We will miss them every day

continued...

There was Derrick who lived in Bay Bulls
And Paul who came from Shearstown
Wade was from Witless Bay
Their spirits will always be around

Allison came from Aquaforté
And Robert the only one to survive
You see miracles do happen
It is a miracle he's still alive
Have angels there to greet them Lord
To show them all the way
Wrap them in your heavenly love
Till families are together again one day.

Never losing their sense of humour, someone once joked, "The Nazis were throwing back what they bought a few years before." Iron ore was once shipped to Germany.

BELL ISLAND TRAGEDY

It was during World War Two
When a thunderous sound of the eruption
Startling this quiet little island
Causing turmoil and deadly destruction

It was nineteen forty-two
When the u-boat first appeared
The ore boats were filled to the brim
Heading to England unaware

The S.S. Rose Castle was the first to sink
Swiftly bringing it down
Realizing their danger they abandoned ship
Only thirteen men were found

The torpedoes were aimed and ready to go
The S.S. Lord Strathcona was in view
But the battery switch didn't work
This gave warning to the ship's crew

There were more attacks to come
The S.S. Saganaga quickly went down
Boats from Lance Cove headed for the scene
In hopes, they too wouldn't drown

The Free French Merchant Ship
In terror, they sent up a flare
This probably was its undoing
Because suddenly it just wasn't there

Four ships went down
All in a matter of weeks
Remembering the bodies afloat
And the sound of the haunting shrieks

> There have been many disasters at sea. This is just one. Two schooners were involved in a collision off Sugar Loaf near Logy Bay.

ARYANN AND SOMERSET DISASTER

A heart-wrenching scene was about to transpire
Involving two schooners Somerset and MaryAnn
A tragedy was about to take place
It was senseless and hard to understand

As witnesses told their story
Grief took its toll in their eyes
Bodies shaking with emotion
Bringing men to their knees of all size

A moderate breeze rippled the water
It was near dawn the moon had just set
Everything seemed clear and visible
No lookout on board the Somerset

Suddenly they were on a collision course
A course they couldn't avoid
Sixteen men and one woman
Were engulfed by the sea and died

This is just one of many
Disasters in the ruthless sea
That shocked a small community
And remains a part of our history

> The collision between The Garland and The Golden Dawn happened in November 1940. Needless mistakes were made that caused many deaths

GARLAND AND THE GOLDEN DAWN

It was November nineteen and forty
The evening was dark but clear
The passengers boarded the Garland
Thinking there was nothing to fear

Miners were spending the weekend
At their homes around Conception Bay
Unequipped and unprepared
Heading back on their way

The Garland left Portugal Cove
About five-thirty in the pm
With the occasional flurry
Saying good-bye to family and friends

Meanwhile on Bell Island
The Golden Dawn was about to leave
Unequipped with the very basics
What happened next it's hard to believe

They both headed on a collision course
About a quarter-mile out to sea
Observing the lights of the Garland
Both ferries could see

Continued...

It became obvious they were going to collide
The Dawn did not give a warning
The sound signal wasn't working
The captains' choices were alarming

They didn't follow procedures
In less than four minutes the Garland went down
And later the Golden Dawn
Needlessly many had drowned

The victims are still remembered
They boarded in the homes on Bell Island
Just one of many tragedies
These Islanders had to withstand

> Many Newfoundlanders never learned to swim. The sea, a dangerous playground filled with undertows and rough water, can instantly change. Many fishermen lost their lives making a meagre living from the sea.

LOST TO A WATERY GRAVE

So many people were lost
Lost to a watery grave
Like a giant hand reaching up
Pulling them into the waves

Some were lost to the November winds
Some were washed overboard
Some just went out fishing
All they found were their boat and oars

Some lost on the Grand Banks of Newfoundland
Some went out in schooners and dories
Some just seem to have disappeared
There are many horrific stories

The sea can be calming and beautiful
But it can be deadly just the same
Be respectful of its powers
Remember the lives that it has claimed.

> The fire started in 1892 in a stable on Freshwater Road. A pipe, dropped by Thomas Fitzpatrick, was said to have caused the fire that devastated St. John's.

ST. JOHN'S FIRE

They say it started in a stable
When Thomas Fitzpatrick dropped his pipe
On July 8th in eighteen ninety-two
On a blustery windy night

The strong winds blew from the northwest
The alarm was sent, the message was clear
The flames engulfed the stable
Dark smoke filled the air

The town's hydrants were said to be useless
Not enough pressure in the mains
The firefighters' labours were futile
Their efforts all in vain

The path of destruction continued
Flames jumping from one structure to another
Buildings were completely gutted
Causing social disorder

The fire subsided the next morning
Much of St. John's was in ruins
All that was left was a city in crumbles
And whiffs of char-filled fumes

Groups of men women and children
With blood-shot eyes and smoke-begrimed faces
Wandering with only the clothes they wore
Homeless bewildered and misplaced

THE CUSTOMS

Newfoundland has many delicious dishes, some derived from the English, with Irish and Welsh influences.

A NEWFOUNDLAND MEAL

Jigs dinner on Sundays
Fish and brews another dish
Roast Capelin in the oven
Fatback poured over fresh fish

Homemade bread every day
Lobster cooked in water from the sea
Cod tongues and scrunchins
A freshly brewed cup of tea

Turnip greens and dandelion leaves
Fish cakes, mussels in a pan
Chips gravy and dressing
Fried bologna a meal fit for a man
Just a few of our Newfy dishes
To test your palate for taste
Cooks all over the world
Have tried and fondly embraced

November 5th is known as "Bonfire Night" or "Guy Fawkes Night". Four hundred years ago, Guy Fawkes was a co-conspirator in the "Gunpowder Plot" of 1605 in England. He and his cohorts planned to blow up the Houses of Parliament in London and kill King James I upon the inaugural opening of Parliament. They succeeded in smuggling several barrels of gunpowder into the basement of the Parliament, but the plot was foiled.

BONFIRE NIGHT

Hide your boats and old tires
Bonfire night will soon be here
They gather up anything that burns
For the largest bonfire of the year

It happens in early November
For months kids would collect
Old tree limbs and harvest materials
Waiting for parents to inspect

We bragged "Ours will be the biggest"
And friends would say the same
Every day we would place something different
To make it the biggest the best with the largest flame

Not knowing the politics of Guy Fawkes
Just having fun was our only desire
And all our friends would gather around
The biggest the best was "our bonfire"

> Keeping traditions alive is the backbone of any culture. One of my favourite times of the year in Newfoundland was when we went Mummering. Oh, what childhood memories it gave us!

JANNIES

They came around at Christmas time
Those creatures of the night
Waiting with anticipation
They looked a dreadful fright

They travelled around from door to door
Calling "Any Jannies allowed in?"
"Yes!" comes a welcome reply
And now the fun begins

Men dressed like women
Women dressed like men
So as not to be recognized
Is it a neighbour or a friend?

Out comes the squeezebox,
They play old jigs and reels
They dance around the kitchen floor
Kicking up their heels

They have a bite to eat
Then a drink of rum
Reminiscing of traditions
Oh it was such fun

Growing up on the Island, there were many traditions. I remember on Valentine's Day we got excited because we would go door to door and slip a special valentine underneath and run away. I remember doing this in Lance Cove, Bell Island.

VALENTINE'S DAY

"Valentine's Day is coming soon"
Our teacher said, "But for today,
Let's draw hearts and colour them
So I could put them on display"

We would colour the hearts and flowers
And print on them 'Please be mine'
And sign it from 'guess who'
Or from 'Your secret valentine'

On the Island I recall
On every Valentine night
We would slip a card under the door
And run and hide with delight

We would go around the neighbourhood
Choose the card we wanted them to have
And hide as they opened the door
Some were funny and made them laugh

We would send the message to the one we loved
Unsigned too shy to let them know
We went back to school the very next day
Never to let it show

> Memories are all we have left at the end, and I have many fond memories of old traditions and culture to pass down to my children and grandchildren.

MUMMERS

*Mummers a tradition I often recall
From young and old alike
Dressing in outrageous costumes
They looked a funny sight*

*They would go from house to house
Calling "Any Jannies allowed in?"
Trying to guess who's under those disguises
Was it a neighbour or a friend?*

*As a child, it was a fun time
A little like Halloween
But we'd have to work for a treat
We would do a little dance or sing*

*These customs have long since passed
I hold these memories dear
It's a shame the next generation
Won't have such treasures to share*

> Yes, I can remember going to visit my Grandmother around the Bay. She made the best homemade bread.

NANNY'S HOMEMADE BREAD

I loved to visit Nanny's house
She made the "best" homemade bread
She would wear her long white apron
And a bandanna around her head

One day she said "Come here child
I will teach you how it's done
It takes a little work
And it's not always fun"

She said "You can stand beside me
And watch me if you wish
Your hands are not yet strong enough"
As she poured some yeast into a dish

She put all the ingredients together
And mixed and punched and kneaded
She moulded a perfect ball of dough
Okay it's time we proceeded

I saw her make the sign of the cross
Pressing it into the risen dough
My mother also did this
The reason I don't know

Oh I can still smell the aroma
As it bakes in the old wood stove
I can taste this delicious homemade bread
That was made with Nanny's love

Newfoundlanders call this the "Capelin scull" and evenings in June and July will find adults and children down on the beaches equipped with buckets and dip nets to gather up this ocean bounty. Traditionally, Capelin fish were spread on gardens as fertilizer. Dried salted Capelin is a traditional Newfoundland snack roasted on a stick over a campfire or in the oven.

THE CAPELIN IS IN

"The Capelin is in" is a phrase I recall
Oh I can almost taste it now
Dad takes the barrels and pails
And spreads the blasty bows

"Grab the nets," mother says
As she stopped to take the frying pan
"Come on let's get going
We want to get as many as we can!"

The water flickered like silver
As the Capelin rolled in droves
Making a sound like rain on pebbles
Abundance with each wave that rolls

We'd squeal with pure delight
As we grab them with bare hands
Mother wound get a fire going
And we'd eat them straight from the frying pan

There are so many memories of home
They hold a special place in my
heart Like a folded corner of a book
Saving them as my bookmark

> Bootlegging and smuggling of hard liquor were common on the Island, especially in the early days of mining. Back then there were over 12,000 people, some of which were thirsty miners.

SMUGGLERS

Bootlegging and smuggling of liquor
Were common in the early days
These thirsty iron ore miners
Would always find a way

While ships were anchored at sea
About a quarter of a mile offshore
Sailors would bring the liquor
Making sure all were accounted for

Local fishermen would trade fish
In return for a flask of rum
Rum for weddings and wakes
Their silence was the rule of thumb

An old schooner called "The Margaret Ann"
Wrecked down by the Scotia pier
The young lads would secretly watch
They would bury and hide the booze there

This went on for many years
While the Customs boat made it's round
There was plenty of rum for the locals
And no one uttered a sound

> Nanny often wore a fancy apron. She had it for special occasions or when company came.

.NANNY'S FANCY APRON

It hangs there on the wall
Over by the stove
It's worn on special occasions
As delicate as any queen's robe

It is Nanny's fancy apron
She wears it when company comes
She fusses around in the kitchen
From stove to table she runs

She wears it to keep her dress clean
And it's sure to catch any spills
Newfoundland is stitched in red
Across the tail embellished frills

Yes I can see Nanny in the kitchen
I can smell those home-cooked meals
Dressed in her fancy apron
Strong memories seem surreal

> Newfoundland has the most wonderful berries I've ever tasted. I remember going blueberry-picking as a child and often ate more then I picked.

THE BLUEBERRY PATCH

I remember when we were kids
We found the perfect blueberry patch
We tried to keep it a secret
So no one could find our stash

It was down a big long meadow
And over the picket fence
Along a winding tree-filled path
We would cover our faces in defence

At the end of the path was the ocean
Guarding a wildflower field
With a hill that was so bountiful
So picturesque and surreal

Bluest of blueberries everywhere
With pails and buckets in hand
We would pick and pick for hours
To sell at our blueberry stand

When we came home our moms could tell
Where we had been all-day
They just had to look at our blue-stained lips
And our empty pail on display

> I remember my mother's clothesline and how proud she was when her line was full and her clothes were as white as the snow.

CLOTHESLINE

You can tell a lot about the people
By the clothes that hang on the line
Flapping in the warm summer breeze
Whitening in the bright sunshine

How many children do they have?
The ages and their gender
Do they have a guest stay there?
Are they heavy set or slender?

A young man's shirt and pants
And Poppy's old wool vest
Nanny's good white apron
A little girl's frilly dress

You can see a soldier's uniform
Hanging proudly on the line
They'll say farewell to the family soon
To fight a war of some kind

Maternity wear lets us know
There is a little one on its way
Yes you can always tell a story
By the clothing on display

> In most homes in Newfoundland, you may find some kind of musical instrument. My father could play the squeezebox and many of his friends loved to hear him play

THE SQUEEZE BOX

He takes the old squeeze box down
And places it gently on his knees
Something magical happens
As he places his fingers on the keys

A twinkle comes to his eyes
A smile comes to his face
The music takes him away
To another time or place

"This was my father's favourite" he'd say
As he plays Nearer My God To Thee
He would play this down in the meadow
Underneath the old apple tree

When my father played his squeeze box
People would come from all around
Just to sit and listen
And to hear the wonderful sound

MYTHS & LEGENDS

> Although the size of the Newfoundland dog can be very intimating, they are very gentle and loving and have saved many lives from the perils of the sea.

THE NEWFOUNDLAND DOG

If you ever see a Newfoundland dog
Just look into its eyes
You'll see a gentle soul
With a heart as big as its size

These water dogs with webbed feet
Born to retrieve and protect
They have saved many lives
From the ocean's fury and wrecks

In eighteen and thirty-two
Many immigrants owed their lives
Without the Newfoundland Dog
They surely wouldn't survive

Saving many from drowning
These lifeguards of the sea
It was said one saved Napoleon Bonaparte
They are a part of history

They deserve a medal of honour
For their bravery love and devotion
These courageous Newfoundland dogs
These water dogs of the ocean

> I remember when I was a child, back in the early fifties, there was talk about a woman in white. I had never seen this ghostly figure and often wondered if this was a made-up story to keep the children home at night. What do you think?

THE WOMAN IN WHITE

Every place has its ghosts and tales
Bell Island had the Woman in White
Many have said they'd seen her
And she only comes out at night

Some say it was a man dressed in white
To scare and to just have fun
They say whenever you see her
The best you can do is to run

She may wait down a long dark lane
Or hide behind some trees
Watch for the woman in white
And steady those shaky knees

I haven't heard if she's still around
But she was when I was a child
Could it be to keep us home at night
The reason she was compiled

> The following was taken from Religious Traditions of the Micmac of Newfoundland. I found it on the Internet and felt this was a story to share.

A TALE ABOUT THE MICMAC AND THE BEOTHUK

Long ago the Micmac and Beothuk were friends
They lived peacefully in St. George's Bay
*The place called Me ski_gtuwi_d*n which means "big gut"*
They travelled in a large canoe every day

t was said that a Micmac boy killed a black weasel
As it was winter, superstition was that it should be white
It was taken to be an omen and misfortune
This tribal volition started a fight

The quarrel was between the two boys
They gathered near the big canoe
The Micmac struck and killed the Beothuk boy
Left his body there in full view

His people soon missed the Beothuk boy
They searched for several days
They found his body near the big canoe
This put them in a warlike rage

The Beothuk were beaten and driven out
For generations, they remained at war
The Micmac continued to live on the outskirts
While the Beothuk kept to the interior

This is the tale from long ago
Whether it's true I cannot tell
I found this story intriguing
You may find it dismal

Some people claim to have seen the fairies. Whenever something unexplained happened they often said the fairies did it. Some still believe the fairies exist today. I have never seen one.

THE FAIRIES

There are tall tales about the fairies
Little men about three feet tall
Mischievous in nature
Luring you with their call

Not everyone has seen them
But there are stories of those who did
One story in particular
Left many scratching their head

Jim had to go into the woods
He was to be gone for just a while
But when he didn't return
His buddies were a little riled

They sent out a small search party
They searched for days and days
When they couldn't find him anywhere
They were baffled and amazed

A few days later he appeared
Wondering why all the fuss
He thought he was gone one hour
You were gone for days you scared us

Then Jim told us a story
About the little people he met
How they fed and entertained him
He swore it was true up until his death

> The Bell Island Mines have been abandoned since the 1960s. Tourists regularly travel to the island to get a peek at what life was like for these Bell Islanders just a half-century ago. But recent trips to the mine have seen tourists and their guides spooked by loud rumblings and flashes of light coming from the deep and dark depths of the underground tunnels.

THE ORYROG

Now that the mines have been abandoned
There are some strange goings-on
Rumblings and flashes of light
They know this doesn't belong

What could be causing these noises
From the darkest depths under the ground
That's scaring the Bell Islanders so bad
It's a spooky and eerie sound

Some say it may be an Oryrog
What is an Oryrog? you ask I
t's a giant dark-haired sheep
It sounds silly don't you laugh

It can stand on its hind legs and breathe fire
And uses a whip to catch its prey
Codfish their favourite food
Some believe they exist today

So when you go near the mines
Listen for an eerie sound
Maybe the Oryrog is hungry
It's coming up from under the ground

I heard that its appetite is huge
Codfish and humans are their favourite meal
If you dare go down the mines
You can let me know if it's real

THE PEOPLE

Humpback Whales, majestic icebergs, sunken ships from the past ...all treasures of our Newfoundland sea. We have many treasures yet to be discovered.

TREASURES OF THE SEA

There are many treasures in our waters
Some are wondrous to see
The thrill of watching the Humpback
Breaching the waves of the mighty sea

There are icebergs in our waters
They take thousands of years to form
Huge enough to sink ships
Shapes magically transformed

There are Harper seals and Hooded seals
Grey seals abundance galore
Devouring smaller species
Skeletal remains washed along the shore

There are sunken ships from World War Two
A goldmine of history preserved
Making our waters valuable
And still there for all to observe

There are many treasures yet to discover
Underneath our Newfoundland sea
Way too many to mention
That stands as part of our history

Dotting the Newfoundland coast are many isolated out-ports, which are communities that were once home to hundreds of people but now lay abandon. Woody Island is a resettled community in Placentia Bay. At one time the community had a population of around 400, but now it is virtually deserted except a few people who return in the summer to fish. and enjoy the relaxing Woody Island Resort.

WOODY ISLAND

Woody Island once was a thriving place
Than a forsaken snapshot in time
With beauty wildlife and waters
Breathtaking landscapes sublime

There is a cozy lodge on the Island
That attracts people from all around
Where you become one with nature
The reverberation of the sea gives a calming sound

Getting away from noise and pollution
The busy thoughts running in your head
Enjoying the peace and serenity
Where both spirits and souls are fed

This little island paradise
Nestled in Placentia Bay
Will take you back in time
Where the whales and dolphins play

The music of Newfoundland's culture
You can't help it but unwind
And the aromas of homemade cooking
Pulls me home to a place and time

> I love to look at old houses when travelling around the Island. They have character and I often wonder about the family that lived there.

THIS OLD HOUSE

There's an old house that stands alone
Its front steps starting to sag
The white picket fence around
Running in a crooked zig-zag

This old house was once a happy one
With children playing in the yard
Young and old were welcomed
An old lilac tree stands guard

This old house has seen many storms
Keeping them sheltered from the rain
Waiting for loved one's return
Waiting but all in vain

The old gate stays halfway open
It creaks now in the breeze
What once were little bushes
Have developed into full-grown trees

This house that stands so wise
Just like prophets of old
Its walls still filled with knowing
Of many things that were never told

> Many Newfoundlanders travel back home continuously. I read somewhere that God can tell a Newfoundlander in heaven because they're the only ones that want to go back home all the time.

WHY DOES THIS ISLAND DRAW ME HOME

Why does this Island keep drawing me back?
Like a magnet that's pulling so strong
I left there many years ago
But my heart still feels the longing

Could it be the sea
The sound of the ocean waves
The jagged rough of the cliffs
Or the underground mining caves

Could it be the stillness
You can hear distant voices on a clear day
Or the smile a friendly nod
Of the friends along the way

Could it be the crisp salty clean air
Or the memories of Nan's homemade bread
Or the simplicity of life back then
Reminiscences I hold in my head

Could it be the traditions
Or the culture that's Newfoundland style
That safe warm environment,
I remember as a child

Whatever it is that calls me back
I know I'll be there one day
To the home, I left so long ago
There my heart will be happy to stay

> I was inspired to write this poem because of my father who spent most of his life underground. There was also added stress on the families, never knowing if their loved ones would come home or if they would be in one piece.

THEY WAIT, THEY WAIT

They wait they wait
Would today seal their fate?
Would the siren blast that dreadful sound?
They wait they wait

Son's brothers and fathers,
Working the mines their allotted toil
Deep in the darkness of the underground
Their skin red from the orey soil

Daughters sisters and mothers,
Each day they silently prayed
That the siren will remain silent
And the inevitable would be delayed

The siren would let them know
Today someone may not come home
They may be trapped inside
Buried and all alone

The women would go about their day
Pretending all is well
Until they see their loved ones
Coming home from the pit of hell

They wait they wait
Would today seal their fate?
Would the siren blast that dreadful sound?
They wait they wait

I remember when the electricity often went out on the Island on cold wintery stormy nights. We felt warm and cozy and safe at home in our beds, covered up in handed down homemade quilts made with love and Nanny's hands.

THE OLD LAMP

The oil lamp hangs on the bedroom wall
How warm and cozy we'd feel
When it was time to say our prayers
By the side of the bed, we would kneel

God bless Mom and Dad
Next came the Lord's Prayer
Bless our friends and family
Bless everyone everywhere

Sinking in our soft feather beds
Making hand shadows on the wall
With a soft glow of the flickering light
Comforting memories I recall

Our imagination would often soar
Making monsters and birds with our hands
With the eerie darkness of the room
They appeared to contract and expand

When cold winter winds blew outside
We'd be warm and cozy in bed
Covered in Nana's homemade quilts
Secure not a care nor a dread

Oh yes my memory takes me back
To the oil lamp on the wall
To a wonderful simpler time
A time I so often recall

> My father worked in the mines for most of his younger years. There were times when he had a strange feeling that just wouldn't go away.

THE MINER

He gets ready to go off to work
It's just like any other day
But he has the strangest feeling
And it just won't go away

He picks up his old metal lunch pail
And kisses his family goodbye
Today seems a little bit different
And he just doesn't understand why

He starts his long journey to work
Seven miles there and back
To number nine iron ore mine
Going down that long lonely track

Armed with a light on a helmet
And a belt to hold his lamp
Wearing a pair of safety boots
Already feeling cold and damp

Going down in the pit of darkness
Crammed in a thirty-man tram
Every face holds a solemn look
As if they're going to the valley of the dammed

They drilled and blasted and loaded
Until nearly the end of the day
"Run!" someone screams
"A cave-in" they heard him say

Continued...

Scattering like rats to find their way
Heading quickly towards the light
The siren blasts to let everyone know
Maybe someone won't be home tonight

He gets ready to go off to work
It's just like any other day
But he has the strangest feeling
And it just won't go away

Almost every home in Newfoundland has been exposed to music or has a member of their family play a musical instrument. We are a province that's, filled with fun and laughter, all of which make Newfoundland a wonderful place to be.

THE MUSIC

Newfoundland is known for its codfish
Also, music that's Newfoundland style
It's traditional representing history and culture
Leaving the past and present beguile

It's been passed down from generation
Old stories from long ago
Maybe told in someone's kitchen
Influenced by abroad continues to grow

Old favourite hymns sung by parents
Old folk tales handed down
The tragedy put to music
Squeezebox and violin creating the sound

With its unique style of tunes
Mixed with a little Irish lingo
Such as our own Harry Hibbs
Who we all come to know

There are many singers and songwriters
Come from our Newfoundland shores
We are proud of every one of them
I'm sure the world will see many many more

In the early 1940s, the Kipawo was sent to Conception Bay to undertake duties of tending anti-submarine nets. At the time German U-Boats were exacting a heavy toll on the iron ore carriers. Several large ships had already been torpedoed before the Kipawo being commissioned in the Royal Navy. We travelled many times on "The Kip" between Portugal Cove and Bell Island.

THE OLD KIP

Kipawo accomplished many purposes,
She was the last of her kind
She carried passengers for years
To the Island to work in the mines

"The Kip" we called her for short
She helped in the time of war
Held a special place for those she served
Guiding ships that carried iron ore

She once was our lifeline
Taking us from the Island to town
She was commissioned by the navy
Tending submarine nets all year round

She was a mighty boat that served us well
And took us across rough seas
Capable of taking many vehicles
She's a part of our Island's history

She is now used as a theatre
This majestic boat is a memory
Some visit now for nostalgia
Recollecting what used to be

> This event had the whole Island buzzing. A moose swam over from the mainland and took over the Island, quickly making himself at home.

BELL" THE MOOSE

In the early morning of eighty-one,
An unusual visitor came to stay
He swam three miles to get here
We wondered if he lost his way

The Islanders heard of this visitor
They came in droves to greet him there
Amid the cheers of the crowd
He climbed the cliff unaware

He explored areas of the island
And disappeared in the deepest of woods
To protect this newfound visitor
Everyone clearly understood

He lived his life as a bachelor
Until a young heifer caught his eye
He battled to keep the males away
The farmers couldn't understand why

You see this guest was a moose they called "Bell"
Mating with cattle was absurd
Did Bell interfere with the cycle of nature
Another moose may be the cure

                                              Continued...

Bell eventually died of a heart attack
At the edge of the old Bell Pond
Many were sad to see him go
For this visitor created a bon

Bell's antlers can be seen at town hall
Where all can pay their respects
And the female cattle graze happily
Recalling the bachelor they'd never forget

My memories often take me back to a time when life was simpler when honour and respect were a part of our being. We were taught at an early age. I sure miss those times.

BACK IN TIME

Let me take you back in time
When the air was fresh and clean
And the sweet sounds of the ocean
Left you peaceful and serene

Let me take you back in time
When family values were strong
When we respected our elders
And we knew right from wrong

Let me take you back in time
When doors were opened wide
Never needing to be locked
Welcoming all inside

Let me take you back in time
Back home when times were good
The smells of homemade bread
And the crackling of firewood

Let me take you back in time
Where your heart does long to be
Childhood memories pulling strong
To the Island in the sea

I have some wonderful childhood memories, growing up on the Island. Times change though and I sometimes wonder if it's for the better. Sometimes I long for the "good old days."

BACK THEN

It seems no matter how long I'm gone
Or wherever I may roam
For in my quiet hours
The sea calls me home

My memories take me back
To a simpler place and time
When the pace of life was slower
And friends weren't hard to find

Our needs were not outrageous
We were content with what we had
Not to outdo our neighbour
Or follow the latest fad

Back then we took the time
To spend with family and friends
Nana and Poppy within reach
The thread that binds and blends

Music filled my soul
Of traditions that are passed
Fundamental memories now
Sadly they never last

> Reminiscing back to "The Good Old Days" I often ask myself, "What happened?" We didn't have much, but we had family, friends, morals, values, and most of all respect for one another.

REMEMBER WHEN

Do you remember years ago?
When morals and values were strong
And families stayed together
Children felt they belonged

When neighbour spoke to a neighbour
A handshake sealed their word
And the thought of using violence
Was absurd

When the only high was on life
Drugs were something prescribed
When children and parents communicated
And their only fight was to survive

Yes times were simple then
Children went to school to learn
There were no dangers back then
And homework their only concern

Maybe it's time we got back
To the way it used to be
Take back morals and values
Where children feel loved and free

> My grandfather fished "The Labrador" in the summer months and he often took my mother to help. She made friends with an Eskimo family. They were called Eskimos back then but now they prefer to be called Inuit.

HER ESKIMO FRIEND

There was an Eskimo family
Mother remembers as a child
And when she'd reminisce
Her lips would crack a smile

She often told us stories
Of her days on "The Labrador"
And of her Eskimo friends
Of the kind of clothing that they wore

Their fathers would fish together
While the kids would be at play
There was a special bond there
That mother still carries to this day

She talked about the house
They stayed in while they were there
Whatever the fathers would catch
Both families would often share

She can still remember their names
Lydia and I would have such fun
While Simon and his father
Would take the Huskies out to run

Those Huskies would always protect them
They would often stand on guard
They would sleep with them at night
And playfully romp in the back yard

Mother still holds those memories dear
She'd love to go back again
Back to the house in Labrador
Back to her Eskimo friends

> The job of the lighthouse keeper, while often isolated and sometimes dangerous especially in earlier times, was to help guide approaching and passing ships of any coastline dangers.

THE LIGHTHOUSE

There is a lighthouse on Bell Island
That performed function during the war
Situated on the eastern part of the Island
From there you can see the Bauline shore

Its light would shine its beacon
To help ships in stormy seas
And guide the little fishing boats
Safely home to their families

The keepers were their guardians
Spending time in lighthouse towers
Keeping watch over twisted coastlines
For many lonely hours

As you climb the narrow staircase
At the top of the spiral stairs
You will see a natural splendour
Releasing of human despair

You'll witness the majestic ocean
Enormous whales peeking up to spray
And the ocean's tapestry of colours
You'll not find in any bouquet

> Thousands of icebergs can be expected to pass down the northern coast from March to July. Their height can be anywhere from 50 to 75 meters.

THE ICEBERGS

They are enormous peeking up towards the sky
The ocean its canvas of display
Nature's glorious work of art
Crispy white floating down the bay

They say it caused the Titanic to sink
These icebergs of Newfoundland
People come to gaze upon this sculpture
As if created by the Master's hand

It's funny how we take things for granted
We would often take a swim
With the Icebergs just yards away
Sparkling as a brilliant gem

For what you see above the water
There's 90% more below
Some as heavy as one hundred thousand tons
And they put on a spectacular show

Yes these towers of beauty
Float slowly and majestically by
What a wondrous piece of nature
A spectacle to passers-by

The" Squeeze Box" is a part of Newfoundland culture. Most families played the squeezebox, which was handed down from father to son or daughter. My father loved to play the squeezebox, but unfortunately, I never learned to play this wonderful instrument.

THE BATTERED OLD SQUEEZE BOX

"This is battered and scarred," said the auctioneer
"I don't know if it's worth my while
To waste time on this old squeeze box"
As he held it up with a smile

"What am I to start this bid?" he cried
"Five, ten, what three?
Three going once three going twice"
"But wait" an old grey-haired man's voice pleaded

"This squeezebox is worth more than three dollars"
He blew the dust off and sat down
And placed the old squeezebox on his knee
And out came the most marvellous sound

His music was as sweet as any orchestra
As if angels joined in and sang
"This squeezebox is priceless"
The voice of the auctioneer rang

"I can't sell this," the auctioneer said
"But I'll loan this to you Old Man
This is meant for you to play
As if it came from the Master's hand"

> Fishing was a way of life for many Newfoundlanders and when it disappeared from overfishing, many boats were left to rot.

MY BOAT

She once was luminous and strong
She guided me through rough seas
Her belly filled to the brim
She was my right hand a part of me

I made her with my own two hands
Carved each board with love
No captain could be prouder
She was as slick as a kid glove

Fishing then was plentiful
Enough food for the winter stored
I kept her clean and painted
She was as shiny as any sword

The times have passed the fish are gone
Huge boats over-fished the sea
Took more than they needed
Now there's hardly any left for me

My boat is a piece of driftwood
Rotted now with time
She just sits there as a reminder
Of the greed that caused this crime

> When the waters became over-fished, the people of Newfoundland were allotted a quota which discouraged many of the young people and caused them to leave feeling hopeless.

THE OLD FISHERMAN

His wrinkled face weathered with time
His hands are callus and red
His body a little bent now
Taking one last look with dread

He has always been a fisherman
He has known no other life
The sea had given him a living
Supporting his children and wife

The young have all gone now
Searching for a better way
Uneducated and old
His only choice is to stay

His boat his prized possession
He takes her out to sea
Reminiscing of the old days
And of times that used to be

No longer can he fish the waters
His age has taken its toll
Now it's old fisherman stories
Stories that have yet to be told

Newfoundlanders are known for their humour and it shows in the names of places that you may see on your visit there. Some signs keep disappearing as visitors want to take them home as souvenirs.

NEWFOUNDLAND PLACE NAMES

In Newfoundland, there are many places
Unique and one-of-a-kind
Nestled by the ocean's blue waters
With miles of alluring coastlines

There's Tickle Cove and Bacon Cove
Blow Me Down and Come By Chance
If you pass by these signs
You may give them a second glance

There's Witless Bay and Conception Bay
Paradise and Sweet Bay
If you think these are strange
Keep reading the signs along the way

There's Berry's Head and Cow Head
Barenaked, Fogo and Jerry's Nose
They may get a little stranger
Just a few more to disclose

There's Cupids, Foxtrap and Gobbies
Happy Adventure and Lawn,
Hey there's many more to come
Just keep reading on

There's Heart's Content, Heart's Delight
Heart's Desire, and Joe Batt's Arm
If you make a joke of these names
You may come to some harm

Continued...

There's Toogood Arm, Snooks Arm
Roberts Arm and Little Seldom,
No matter which place you go
They're sure to make you welcome

There's Deadman's Cove and Nameless Cove
Herring Neck and Mosquito
We are almost at the end of our journey
There are just a few more signs to go

There's Spanish Room and Nippers Harbour
Red Head Cove and Noggin Cove
Little Heart's Ease and River Of Ponds
Just a few place names you'll love

AFTER THE MINES

Many homes stood vacant
After the mines closed down
They just walked away and left
Feeling defeated, and letdown

My Parents left the only home they've known
Leaving friends, and family behind
Moving to unfamiliar territories
Fear of the unknown filled their mind

Not everyone understood their ways
Their dialect, would be the blunt of jokes
But they took it all in stride
They were not easily provoked

My father could barely read
Or even write his name
He hid his humiliation
And his feelings of shame

They tackled many challenges
Facing them day by day
Newfoundlanders are resilient
They just... seem to be built that way

> Bell Island was Canada's longest operating mining project. They shipped Iron Ore to Canada, United States, West Germany, Belgium and Holland.

THE MINES ARE CLOSING

The news travelled quickly
The mines are closing down
To the horror of Bell Islanders
And workers, from all around

This caused such great concern
What will the future hold?
Life as they knew it, would change
The effect was yet to unfold

The financial stress was plain to see
Stores would be closing down
Some families left the Island
Some moved to the nearest town

The young left to find work
The elders chose to stay
The effect of the mines closing down
Is still felt to this very day

But the Islanders are resilient
Using the land and sea
And finding work elsewhere
Some stayed, and raised their family

When the terrorist attracts occurred in 2016, many planes were detoured and landed in Newfoundland. Many lives were changed and many friends were made out of this tragedy

TERRORIST ATTACK

It was 2016 the world held their breath
The world trade Center fell
Terrorist attack was upon us
The pentagon was hit as well

The US shut down their airspace
Stranding thousands of people in the air
The captain announced the changes
The passengers were kept unaware

We have to land in Gander
No one heard of this secluded place
They sat on the tarmac for hours
Feeling a little confused and misplaced

The Newfoundlanders were busy behind the scenes
Preparing to take care of the crowds
But never expected for one minute
Many more planes would peek through the clouds

They fed and clothed the strangers
And made them feel at home
They attended to their every need
Even let them use their phoned

Many lives were lost from the attack
When evil showed its ugly head
But for the people that landed in Gander
They knew they had nothing to dread

The world soon learned about Newfoundland
Their culture and their ways
The friendships they made
Remains ...till this very day

OLD DITTIES

> I bet you can think of a few old ditties or sayings that were handed down in your family!

The world is round
The sea is deep
In your arms, I like to sleep
In your bed, I'd like to lie
With no one there but you and I

Mother, can I go out to play?
Yes, my darling daughter Keep
your petticoat over your knees
And don't go near the water

Little Dickey Doubt
Does your mother know you're out?
With your hands in your pocket
And your shirttail out

May your home be full of roses
And your bed full of joy
First to fill the cradle
Be a bouncing baby boy
If his hair is full of curls
I wish you than a baby girl

Uncle Joe Drover
From Island Cove came
With hatchet and hammer
Chisel and plane
Wind from the west came unto blow
Uncle Joe Drover got bogged in the snow

First of March was very tough
Uncle Billy lost his cuff
He warmed his hands in Susan's frock
He found his cuff in Jones' dock

Dan, Dan the funny old man washed
his face in the frying pan Combed
his hair with the leg of the chair,
Dan, Dan the funny old man

OLD SAYINGS

My mother oftencomes up with old ditties and sayings. I would like to share some with you.

Me dear, what happened? You look like a birch broom in the fits. (Bad hair day)

Stop your skylarking. (Stop fooling around) Go on wit ya! (No kidding)

What ya at bye? (What are you doing?)

Go quick, and come quick and stay a long time. (Time is a wasting)

You're as crooked as a dog's hind legs. (In a bad mood)

You have a belly on you like a harbour tomcod (You have put on a little weight)

Who d'ya belongs to bye? (Who are your parents) Knock it off, would ya? (Stop it will you)

Gobsmacked (Speechless)

Come day, go day, God send Sunday. (Thank God for Sundays, a day of rest)

Go home and tell your mudder she's got lassie buns. (Send an annoying child home)

Stay where you're to and I'll come where you're at. (Stay there, I'm on my way)

Continued...

Coopy down and pick that up, would ya? (Bend down and pick that up) submitted by Dell Hutchings

Scuff your shoes before you come in (Clean your shoes)

Out gallivanting. (Out and about
Crossed knives on the table. (You'll fight)

Buy a broom in May. (You'll sweep your friends away)

Itchy foot. (You're going to walk on strange ground)

Arn s'marnin? Narn s'marnin. (Any fish this morning? No fish this morning) submitted by Johnny Lomond

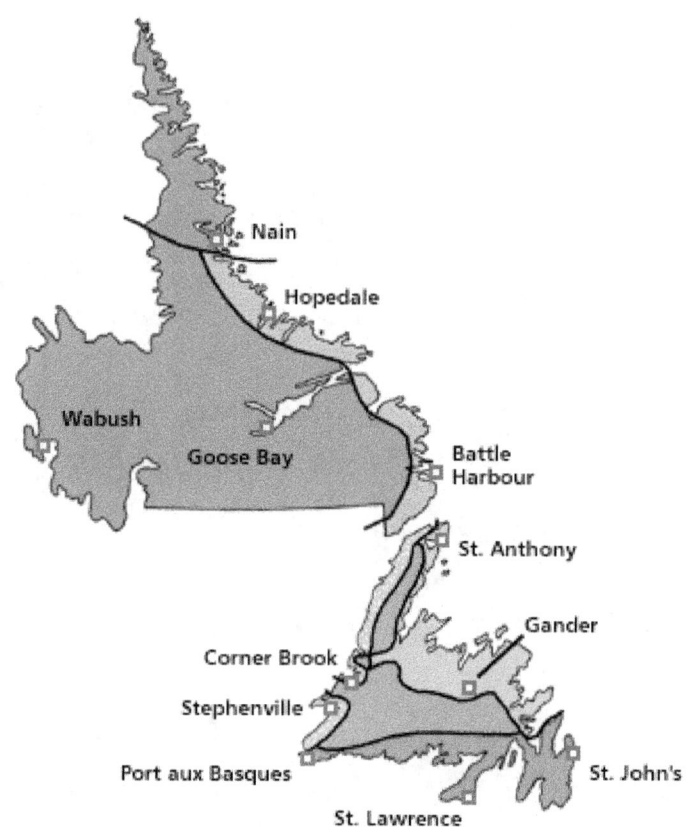

www.ingramcontent.com/pod-product-compliance
Lightning Source LLC
Chambersburg PA
CBHW050606300426
44112CB00013B/2104